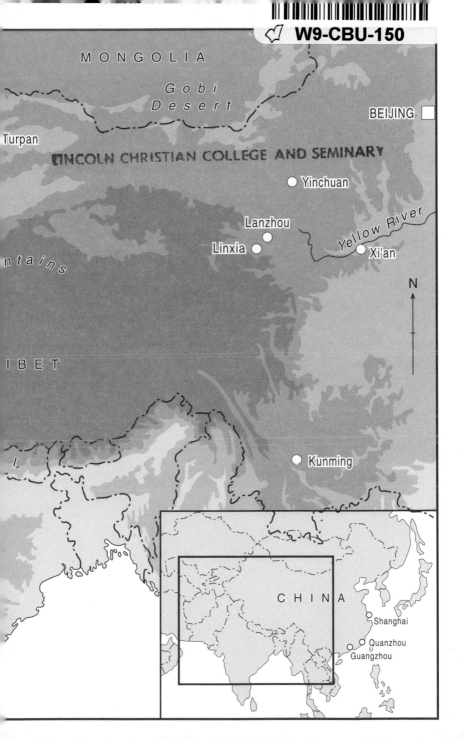

MONGOLIA

Gobi
Desert

BEIJING

Turpan

Yinchuan

Lanzhou

Linxia

Yellow River

Xi'an

N

ntains

IBET

L

Kunming

CHINA

Shanghai

Quanzhou

Guangzhou

IMAGES OF ASIA

China's Muslims

Series Editors, China Titles:

NIGEL CAMERON, SYLVIA FRASER-LU

China's Muslims

MICHAEL DILLON

HONG KONG
OXFORD UNIVERSITY PRESS
OXFORD   NEW YORK
1996

Oxford University Press

Oxford New York
Athens Auckland Bangkok Bogota
Bombay Buenos Aires Calcutta Cape Town
Dar es Salaam Delhi Florence Hong Kong Istanbul
Karachi Kuala Lumpur Madras Madrid Melbourne
Mexico City Nairobi Paris Singapore
Taipei Tokyo Toronto

and associated companies in
Berlin Ibadan

Oxford is a trade mark of Oxford University Press

First published 1996
This impression (lowest digit)
1 3 5 7 9 10 8 6 4 2

Published in the United States
by Oxford University Press, New York

British Library Cataloguing in Publication Data
available

Library of Congress Cataloging-in-Publication Data

Dillon, Michael, 1949–
China's Muslims / Michael Dillon.
p. cm. — (Images of Asia)
Includes bibliographical references and index.
ISBN 0-19-587504-4 (hc : alk. paper)
1. Muslims — China. I. Title. II. Series.
DS731. M87D55 1996
951'.008'82971—dc20 96-11508
CIP

Printed in Hong Kong
Published by Oxford University Press (China) Ltd
18/F Warwick House, Taikoo Place, 979 King's Road,
Quarry Bay, Hong Kong

Contents

95860

Acknowledgements

I am grateful to colleagues in the Chinese Academy of Social Sciences, Beijing, and in particular to Huang Tinghui and other researchers at the Institute of Nationalities Research, for useful discussions and help in obtaining books and articles on China's Muslims. In Ningxia, I was greatly assisted by Muhammed Uisar Yang Huaizhong and his staff at the Ningxia Academy of Social Sciences, Yinchuan, and especially by Sharif Wang Yongliang, who helped me with travel arrangements to the smaller Hui towns in Ningxia and introduced me to people I would not otherwise have been able to meet. Liu Jianyi, formerly of the Xinjiang Academy of Social Sciences, travelled with me to Turpan and Changji, and his fluent Uyghur was invaluable during those visits.

There are few scholars conducting research on China's Muslim communities, and particularly few based in Europe, so I am pleased to be able to acknowledge discussions with Wang Jianping of the University of Lund, Elizabeth Alles of Paris, and Dietmar Federlein of Erlangen University. Each of these individuals has been very gracious in helping to confirm or reject interpretations of Sino-Muslim history and society.

Funding for my visits to China was made available by the British Academy and the Economic and Social Research Council's exchange programme with the Chinese Academy of Social Sciences, the Universities' China Committee in London, and the Staff Travel Fund and the Department of East Asian Studies of the University of Durham. I am grateful to all for their assistance.

Chronological Table of the Chinese Dynasties

Xia	c.2100–c.1600 BC
Shang	c.1600–c.1027 BC
Western Zhou	c.1027–771 BC
Eastern Zhou	770–221 BC
Spring and Autumn period	770–476 BC
Warring States period	475–221 BC
Qin	221–207 BC
Han	206 BC–AD 220
Three Kingdoms	220–280
Western and Eastern Jin	265–420
Northern and Southern Dynasties	420–589
Sui	581–618
Tang	618–907
Five Dynasties	907–960
Song	960–1279
Jin	1115–1234
Yuan	1271–1368
Ming	1368–1644
Qing	1644–1911
Republic of China	1912–1949
People's Republic of China	1949–

1

Muslim China

FEW PEOPLE outside China are aware of the presence of Muslims in the Middle Kingdom, although China's Islamic population may be as large as twenty million. Even within the country many Han Chinese, the majority ethnic group, have very little real knowledge of their Muslim neighbours. Most of these Muslims are members of families and lineages which can trace their religious heritage back through many centuries. Many of them live in villages, towns, urban neighbourhoods, and even whole regions in which the dominant culture has for centuries been Islamic rather than Chinese. Muslim communities, with their mosques, *madrasa*, halal butchers and food stalls, and many other distinctive features, are found in almost every part of China, from the southern coastal provinces of Guangdong and Fujian, where the first Muslims to visit China came as sailors and merchants, to the far north-eastern provinces of Liaoning and Heilongjiang. The capital, Beijing, has its own long-standing Muslim quarter in the area around the Niujie (Ox street) Mosque, but there at least forty other mosques in the city. Far in the south-west, Yunnan has a large and influential Muslim population that is part of the complex ethnic patchwork in that province.

Islam and its highly visible culture have left the deepest impressions in China's remote north-west, along what has become known as the Silk Road—the ancient system of trading routes affording access to Central Asia, the Middle East, and Europe. It is on that region, the present-day provinces of Gansu, Qinghai, and Shaanxi and the autonomous regions of Ningxia and Xinjiang, that this account will concentrate. North-western China has had a

complex history, as ancient remains still visible today tes-
tify. Over the centuries it has been home to speakers of
the Tibetan, Turkic, Mongolian, and Chinese language families. Evidence of the Manichaean, Nestorian, and Buddhist
beliefs that preceded Islam survives in works of art such
as the Buddhist cave shrines of Maijishan, in southern
Gansu province, and the cave paintings of Bezeklik, just
off the road between Urumqi and Turpan in Xinjiang. The
eerie ruined cities of Gaochang and Jiaohe in the Turpan
basin are redolent of ancient pre-Islamic civilizations. It
was in this intricate cultural, religious, and ethnic matrix
that many of the most important developments of Islam
in China took place.

It is no accident that Muslim communities and cultures
are more distinctive and highly developed in China's north-
west than in other parts of the country, for it is this region
that is closest to the Central Asian and Middle Eastern origins of Chinese Islam. In many ways the existence of these
communities can be regarded as an extension of mainstream Central Asian culture into China. Mainstream Central
Asia consists of the states of Uzbekistan, Turkmenistan,
Tajikistan, Kyrgyzstan, and Kazakhstan. The independent
Muslim khanates which ruled these lands were conquered
by Russia and incorporated into the Russian empire during the nineteenth century. The states as they exist today
were created as separate Soviet Socialist Republics under
Stalin's government as a means of controlling their Turkic-
and Iranian-speaking populations, and they have achieved
a measure of independent statehood since the collapse of
Soviet power in 1991.

Most of Xinjiang, ruled by the Chinese state since the
power of the Qing dynasty was extended westward during
the eighteenth century under the rule of the Qianlong
emperor (r. 1736–96), is clearly Central Asian in language,

religion, and culture, and the neighbouring regions of Gansu, Qinghai, Ningxia, and Shaanxi have been profoundly affected by Central Asian civilization.

Today, Central Asian culture, subsumed for more than a century into a generalized imperial Russian, and later Soviet, identity, still remains relatively unknown outside of a small circle of specialists. Russian became the language of the empire, and subsequently of the whole Soviet Union, and displaced many of the minority languages. The Muslims of Central Asia were discouraged from retaining their traditional languages and cultures, since these were so closely connected with Islam. Muslim beliefs were intolerable both to the imperial Russian state, based on the Orthodox church, and to its successor, the Soviet Union, which promoted atheism. The very existence of Muslim communities often was regarded as a threat to the unity of the state. Consequently, Central Asian cultures were severely damaged by a process of Russification.

Some explanation of the term Muslim, as it is used in this book and by the Chinese authorities, is necessary. Since the People's Republic of China was established in October 1949, there has been no systematic attempt by the central government to calculate the number of followers of Islam, or, indeed, of any other religion. For much of the period since 1949, it was state and party policy to promote atheism and to suppress or ignore religions, which were regarded as feudal and medieval superstitions. This uncompromising approach was modified in more liberal times, notably since 1979, to allow the limited expression of religious beliefs provided that these did not conflict with the interests of the state. This positive development was primarily a concession to the rights of ethnic minorities and their beliefs, rather than an indicator of a more favourable attitude towards religious freedom.

Although religious leaders in China have their own esti-
mates of the numbers of their followers, they do not have
the resources that the state has at its disposal to compile
statistics. State organizations have kept records of the population of different ethnic minority groups, in line with the
nationalities policy that the Chinese Communist Party
adapted from the practices of Stalin's Soviet Union. Ten
nationalities (*minzu*, in Chinese) have been identified as
Muslim, either because of their tradition and culture or
their current religious adherence, and Chinese accounts of
Muslims apply the term equally to all members of those
ten nationalities. The degree to which China's Muslims
would be considered pious believers by the rest of the
Islamic world varies greatly. There are imams and their
loyal followers in the mosques whose practices are the
same as orthodox Muslims anywhere in the Islamic world,
and there are also devoted members of secretive Sufi brotherhoods who remember Allah through chanting and dancing.
On the other side, there are Communist Party cadres from
the ethnic groups designated as Muslim who are at least
officially atheist. Many members of China's Muslim communities find themselves somewhere between these two
positions.

Various criteria are used for assigning individuals and
communities to the officially recognized ethnic groups in
China, but an important one is the language that they
speak. Six of the ten Muslim ethnic groups, whose members live mainly in the Xinjiang Autonomous Region (known
also as Eastern Turkestan to many non-Chinese), are the
Uyghurs, Kazakhs, Kyrgyz, Uzbeks, and Tatars, each of
whom speak a language from the Turkic family, and the
Tajiks, whose tongue is related closely to Persian. In the
region that borders Gansu and Qinghai provinces, there are
three smaller Muslim groups, the Salars, the Bao'an, and

the Dongxiang. The Salars speak a Turkic language which some linguists consider to be merely a dialect of Uyghur. The Bao'an and Dongxiang languages are archaic forms of Mongolian, heavily influenced by Chinese through centuries of contact. Of all the Muslim ethnic groups, perhaps the most intriguing are the Hui, who are predominantly Chinese speakers.

The Hui

The term Hui, sometimes seen as Huihui, has been used in different periods as both the name of an ethnic group and as a description of religious adherence, simply denoting Muslim, and it is not always clear from the sources which meaning is intended. In contemporary China it is a portmanteau word, a category which includes all Muslims not otherwise accounted for by ethonyms like Uyghur or Kazakh. Unlike the other Muslim groups, Hui have settled all over China in large numbers and can be found in every province and almost every town and city. However, there are significant concentrations of Hui people in two regions of north-western China: in Gansu province, where an area to the west of the capital, Lanzhou, is designated the Linxia Hui Autonomous Prefecture, and in Ningxia (Fig. 1.1), once a part of Gansu but in 1958 designated a Hui autonomous region, a level of administration equivalent to that of a province. According to the 1990 census, the total Hui population of China was 8,602,978.

Hui Muslims are distinguished from members of other Muslim communities in China by their language. Uyghurs, Kazakhs, and other groups which have an Islamic background have their own Turkic (or in the case of the Tajiks, Iranian) language, whereas the Hui for the most part use

5

1.1 Hui men working in the village of Najiahu, south of Yinchuan.

the regional form of Chinese that prevails where they live or where their community originated. They continue to use a large number of Arabic and Persian words, however, and preserve an attachment to the Arabic script for decorative and symbolic as well as for religious purposes.

It is difficult to make accurate generalizations about the Hui, as there are great regional variations in their history and culture. In particular, there are significant differences between the Hui communities in Gansu and Ningxia, in China's north-west, where Islam is closely woven into the fabric of everyday life, and the Hui inhabitants of the cities of Quanzhou and Changzhou in Fujian province on the south-eastern coast. Members of the latter group, paradoxically, display a less-pronounced Islamic character and have assimilated more closely with the local Han population, in spite of the fact that their Muslim identity goes back much further than that of the communities of the north-west.

The Uyghurs

The Uyghurs (Fig. 1.2) consider themselves to be the indigenous people of Xinjiang, where the majority of them live, although there are Uyghurs in Kazakhstan and other parts of the former Soviet Union and small émigré communities in Turkey and Germany. They probably arrived in Xinjiang as part of the great westward migration of Turkic peoples from what is now Mongolia in the eighth and ninth centuries. The total Uyghur population of Xinjiang today is approximately seven million. Their language is related to Turkish, but it is sufficiently different to make the two

1.2 Uyghur man bringing sheep to the market at Kashghar.

mutually incomprehensible. In addition to their identity as Uyghurs, most tend to identify themselves by the oasis town from which they originate, such as Kashghar, Yarkand, Karghalik, or Turpan.

Uyghurs have become highly skilled at oasis agriculture, making the most effective use of the meagre supply of water available to them. This involvement in settled agriculture distinguishes them from most of the other Turkic-speaking peoples of the region, like the Kazakhs and Kyrgyz, who remain largely nomadic pastoralists. Indeed, the Uyghurs are often known by the name *taranchi* (cultivator), after the eighteenth-century Uyghurs sent from southern Xinjiang to Ili (Ghulja), near the border with Kazakhstan, to work as farmers and border guards. Uyghur oases in southern Xinjiang and the grape-growing Turpan region east of Urumqi are irrigated by a complex system of *kariz* wells supplied by underground watercourses which channel the melting snow from the mountains and bring it to the fields with a minimum of evaporation.

A group of Uyghurs who migrated into Gansu in the ninth century speak a variety of the Uyghur language influenced by Mongolian and Chinese and not now intelligible to the Uyghurs of Xinjiang. They are known as Yellow Uyghurs and have remained Buddhists, being far enough east to have avoided Islamization.

The Kazakhs

The Kazakhs of Xinjiang are essentially the same people as the inhabitants of the neighbouring state of Kazakhstan, formerly a Soviet republic. Many families have relatives on both sides of the border, to a large extent the result of the great migration of 1962, when Kazakhs fled Xinjiang to avoid the programme of collectivization being implemented as part of China's Great Leap Forward. Chinese and Soviet Kazakhs continued to be separated after this time by the Sino–Soviet dispute, which began in 1960 but became public knowledge three years later. The dispute effectively closed the borders between China and its Central Asian neighbours. After the collapse of Soviet power in 1991, however, old relationships were re-established and families which had been divided for more than thirty years were reunited.

Traditionally, Kazakhs were herdsmen and stockbreeders, rather than agriculturalists like the Uyghurs, and their lifestyle, culture, and physical appearance are close to those of the Mongols. Kazakh mythology claims that they are descendants of Genghis (in Mongolian, Chinggis) Khan. There is also a Kazakh minority community in the west of Mongolia. The total Kazakh population of China, almost all of whom live in Xinjiang, was recorded by the 1990 census as 1,111,718.

Kazakh, like Uyghur, is a Turkic language and was also traditionally written in the Arabic script as modified for Persian. This script was replaced by the Cyrillic in the Soviet Union and by Latin script in China in the 1960s, but Kazkah-language publications in China gradually reverted to the Arabic script during the 1980s. In Kazakhstan, where few urban Kazakhs speak the language with any degree of fluency, it has been largely displaced by Russian, and many Kazakhs in search of a post-Soviet identity look to the Kazakh community in Xinjiang, with which they are once again in contact, to revitalize their culture.

The Kyrgyz

The semi-nomadic Kyrgyz are spread throughout western and southern Xinjiang, but there is a significant concentration in the Kizilsu Kyrgyz Autonomous Prefecture, set in the foothills of the Tianshan range which separates them from their kin in the former Soviet republic of Kyrgyzstan. Most Kyrgyz are herdsmen, tending flocks of sheep and camels and, like the Kazakhs, they moved their animals across the mountains according to the season until the Sino–Soviet dispute closed the border. Their language and customs are closely related to those of their Kazakh neighbours.

The Uzbeks

China's Uzbeks, close relatives of the native population of Uzbekistan and the Uzbeks of Afghanistan, can be found throughout southern and western Xinjiang. The Uzbeks originate in the great Central Asian oases of Samarkand, Bukhara, and Tashkent and probably moved into present-day Xinjiang in the eighteenth century. Like the Uyghurs, they are predominantly farmers, and there are concentrations of urban Uzbeks in Ili, Kashghar, Shache, Yecheng, and the provincial capital of Urumqi, among other cities in the region. According to the 1990 census, the Uzbek population of China was only 14,502, greatly outnumbered by the Uyghurs.

Uzbeks in Xinjiang have lived in close proximity to Uyghurs for so many generations that there is little difference in lifestyle, food, clothing, or religious practices between the two groups. The Uzbek language is used within their community, but most are fully conversant with

Uyghur, which is very similar in its vocabulary and structure to Uzbek, and use this language outside their own communities.

The Tatars

The group classified as Tatars, with only 4,872 members registered in the 1990 census, is one of the smallest ethnic groups in China. Most live in northern Xinjiang, near the border with Kazakhstan, and are pastoralists.

The Salars

The Salars are an ethnic group speaking a Turkic language who trace their ancestry back to migrants who arrived from the Samarkand region during the Ming dynasty (1368–1644). Salar storytellers tell of two brothers who left Samarkand some time during the Mongol conquests in search of a new home. Leading a white camel, which had on its back containers filled with water, soil from their native land, and a copy of the Koran, they travelled along the Silk Road towards China until they arrived at Xunhua, in the eastern part of Qinghai province. They settled in what the local Chinese regarded as inhospitable and uncultivatable hills but which the Salars found similar to the environment from which they had come.

Over the centuries, the Salars have acquired a reputation for fierceness which persists to the present day, and many have followed military careers. Others traded by raft down the dangerous rivers or by caravan across the high plains and deserts. The Xunhua that the ancestors of the Salars found in the thirteenth century was inhabited mainly by

11

Mongols, but there were also settlements of other Muslim communities, who would later become part of the Hui group, as well as Tibetans and Han Chinese. Fewer than one thousand Salars formed the original community, and although they intermarried with the Hui and other Muslims (although not with the Han), they retained their language and are regarded as closer to Central Asian culture than are other Muslims in China. In 1990, there were 87,697 people classified as Salars, the vast majority of them still living in Xunhua where their ancestors originally settled.

The Bao'an

The Bao'an, or Bonan in their own language, are a small Muslim ethnic group only accepted as a separate nationality in March 1952. They had previously been known as the Bao'an Hui and treated as members of the Hui nationality. Only 12,212 people were registered as Bao'an in the 1990 census and almost all live in a small area in the southwest of Gansu province. They trace their origins to groups of Mongol and Central Asian troops sent out during the Yuan dynasty (1271–1368) to garrison and cultivate the border town of Tongren in present-day Qinghai province. The original migrants intermarried with local Tibetans, Han Chinese, and other minority groups living in the surrounding hills. The Bao'an language is related to archaic forms of Mongolian but has many borrowings from Chinese.

The Dongxiang

There has been little detailed investigation of the Dongxiang people and their history, and there is uncertainty about their origin. Some scholars trace their origins to Mongol troops who were brought in to garrison the city of Linxia, at the western edge of present-day Gansu province, as the Mongols consolidated their conquest of China in the thirteenth century. These troops are said to have converted to Islam in the sixteenth century. Others argue that they are the descendants of Muslim Sardars or Sarts brought into China by the armies of Genghis Khan as they returned from the great expedition into Central Asia at the beginning of the Mongol dynasty. They became known as Dongxiang, which translates as 'eastern village', because most lived in the mountains east of Linxia, but their own name for themselves is Santa. Almost all of the 373,872 Dongxiang registered in the census of 1990 live in what has now been designated the Dongxiang autonomous county, where they are mostly farmers.

The Dongxiang language belongs to the Mongolian language family. It has archaic features similar to those of Bao'an and many loan words borrowed from Chinese, Arabic, Persian, and Turkic languages.

The Tajiks

The Tajik population of China, largely confined to the Tashkorgan region of south-western Xinjiang, amounts, according to the 1990 census, to 333,538 persons. Tajiks speak a language related to Persian, as do their kindred in Tajikistan and northern Afghanistan. Some Tajik communities live in seclusion high in the Pamirs and have retained their Ismaili Shi'a faith, which exists nowhere else in Chinese Islam.

As with the definitions of ethnic groups everywhere, the designations of these nationalities are far from settled, and their use in China has often been criticized as crude and mechanical. There is much disagreement over the accuracy of the classifications, and there are many examples of individuals and communities with ethnically mixed backgrounds, but Muslims in China commonly identify themselves and each other by use of these names. The unique characteristics of each of the different Muslim groups are best explained in terms of the history of each community's evolution, beginning with the story of its founders' migration into China and exploring its members' interaction with the Chinese population among whom they have lived and worked.

2

The Origins and Characteristics of Chinese Islam

ON THE WHOLE, China's Muslims are not ethnic Chinese converts but are the descendants of Muslims from the Middle East and Central Asia who migrated to China at various times and for various reasons. Some were voluntary migrants, while others were taken to the Middle Kingdom as slaves or bondsmen.

Islam appeared in China very soon after the religion's founding by the Prophet Muhammad in the Arabian cities of Mecca and Medina during the seventh century AD. At the time, China was in transition from the short-lived Sui dynasty (AD 581–618), which had reunited the country after the divisions of the period known as the Northern and Southern dynasties, to the Tang (618–907). The Tang dynasty is universally recognized as one of the greatest eras of Chinese civilization: prosperous, well-administered, and open to outside influences. It was a period which produced great art. Painting, sculpture, architecture, poetry, literary criticism, and scholarship all flourished.

The year AD 622, the date of the Hegira, the migration of the Prophet Muhammad from Mecca to Medina, which became year one in the Islamic lunar calendar, was the fifth year of the reign of the founding emperor of the Tang dynasty, Tang Gaozu. The first emperor's personal name was Li Yuan, and the Li family, who were to rule throughout the dynasty, had mixed Chinese and Central Asian origins in spite of the apparently pure Chinese names they used. Tang culture was influenced profoundly by this link with the steppe and desert peoples to the west of China.

Chinese scholars searching historical sources to find the earliest record of Muslims in China have arrived at several possible dates. Some of the sources, apparently accounts simply of travellers from the countries that would eventually become Muslim, even predate the foundation of Islam. Visitors from distant lands mostly entered Tang China by two main routes: overland across Central Asia, along what was to become known as the Silk Road, and by sea to south-eastern China, an approach now called the Spice Route, as most of its travellers were merchants seeking spices from the islands of South-East Asia. Ambassadors, Nestorian Christian and Buddhist missionaries, and traders from Central Asia and India came by land to the Tang capital, Chang'an, near the city known today as Xi'an. During periods of expansion of the Tang empire, captured prisoners of war, many of them Turks from Central Asia who were not yet Islamized, were brought back to China and enslaved.

Along the maritime trade route came merchants, many of whom settled in the port cities and trading centres of the south-eastern coast. Quanzhou, Changzhou, and Guangzhou (Canton) all became celebrated commercial centres. The visitors from the Middle East who traded and later settled in these cities are usually known as Arab merchants, but there is strong evidence to suggest that they were of mixed ethnic and religious origins. There were Jews and Nestorian Christians as well as Muslims among them, and their common language was probably Persian rather than Arabic. Temporary trading outposts evolved into permanent settlements, and these were the first source of the present Muslim population of China. In Quanzhou there are still hundreds of gravestones with inscriptions in Arabic, Persian, and Chinese, marking the lives and deaths of Muslims from the Yemen, Persia, and Central Asia.

The second source of China's Muslim population can be found in a series of events usually considered to be a catastrophe for Asian and European communities alike: the Mongol conquests of the thirteenth century. The composition of China's population was profoundly affected by the political and social changes brought about by the conquest, as can be seen from the accounts of the origins of the various ethnic groups given in the preceding chapter. On their expeditions westward to conquer Central Asia, the armies of Genghis Khan and his successors sacked major Islamic centres, including Bukhara and Samarkand, and transported sections of the population—skilled armourers, other craftsmen, and enslaved women and children among them—back to China, where they were settled as servants to Mongol aristocrats.

When in 1271 the Mongols established the Yuan dynasty to rule China, they used Central Asians as border guards, tax collectors, and administrators, finding them more reliable than the Han Chinese population they had conquered. In the Mongol perception of Chinese society, Mongols were the élite, but the *semu* (coloured eyes) from the steppes of Central Asia came next in the hierarchy and were considered superior to both the Han Chinese population and the non-Chinese minorities who lived in southern China. Although it is impossible to be certain of the numbers of Central Asians who were moved into China at this time, it is clear that they far outnumbered the Muslims who had settled in China before the Mongol conquests, particularly in northern China. It may be said that the Mongol conquest was the single most important factor in the creation of important Muslim communities in China.

It was during the Ming dynasty that the Muslim population of China first became a permanently settled community. The Ming dynasty, founded by Zhu Yuanzhang, the leader of the most successful anti-Mongol resistance forces, is usually portrayed as a Chinese dynasty, in contrast to the Mongol dynasty which preceded it and the Qing dynasty of the Manchus which succeeded it, both of which are deemed barbarian regimes. In reality, Ming China was a multi-ethnic society with Muslims of Central Asian origin again playing a prominent role as tax collectors, administrators, and traders, but serving under Chinese rather than Mongol jurisdiction.

The Ming government had an enlightened view of different religions. Islam was tolerated and missionaries from Central Asia and Arabia made their way into the country. Nanjing, the first Ming capital, became celebrated as a centre of Islamic learning and culture: Wang Daiyu, the most illustrious Islamic scholar of all time in China, wrote the influential *Zhengjiao zhenquan* (Righteous commentary on the true religion) and other religious treatises in that city. Ming Taizu, as the dynasty's founding emperor was known after his death, sent Muslim troops to garrison the distant frontiers of his empire, thus establishing the Hui communities of Gansu and Ningxia in the north-west and Yunnan in the south-west.

The Ming dynasty was a period of remarkable economic and social change, during which the economy became more commercialized and handicraft arts reached a pinnacle. The empire fell into decline during the seventeenth century, however, when over-taxation and famine provoked insurrection, and political factionalism and corruption weakened the central government. In 1644, armies of the Manchu confederacy entered Beijing, the capital of the collapsing regime, and established their own administration, which they named the Qing. Manchu emperors and their nobles, becoming progressively more Chinese in their culture and outlook but still regarded by many Han Chinese as alien conquerors, ruled China until the imperial era finally ended in 1911.

During the Qing dynasty, China's Muslims began to acquire a reputation as a fierce and rebellious minority. There was sporadic resistance to the Qing conquest in the late seventeenth century, but it was in the late nineteenth century, during three outbreaks of bitter and brutal communal violence usually known as the Muslim rebellions, that this reputation was confirmed. From 1855 to 1873, Muslims in Yunnan rebelled and their leader, Du Wenxiu, declared himself the ruler of an independent Muslim sultanate. The insurrection in Shaanxi and Gansu, which occurred between 1862 and 1878, ravaged the whole of north-western China. As a result, the Hui Muslim population was drastically reduced and faced the real possibility of extinction. From 1867 to 1877, the region around Kashghar and part of northern Xinjiang was ruled as an independent state after the rebellion led by Yakub Beg. More recently, conflict between Muslims and local Han landlords and officials led to a further period of serious disorder on the Gansu and Qinghai border in 1895. These insurrections devastated the border regions of China and left behind a legacy of mutual suspicion between Muslims and Han Chinese. Chinese officials have feared the possibility of Muslim separatism ever since.

Religious Traditions

The vast majority of Muslims in China regard themselves as orthodox Sunni Muslims who follow the Hanafi school of law, thus placing themselves firmly in the mainstream tradition of Islam. In China, this mainstream Islam is referred to as *gedimu*, which is simply the Chinese transliteration of the Arabic *al qadim*, 'the ancient'. It is the oldest established tradition within Chinese Islam.

There has been some controversy and confusion about other sects in Chinese Islam. During the late nineteenth and early twentieth centuries, the most influential Western students of Islam in China were missionaries who reasoned that Muslim Chinese, already committed to the worship of one god, might be easier to convert to Christianity than the polytheistic Buddhist and Daoist believers among the Han population. These missionaries were aware of different groups within the Muslim community, known by names such as the Old Teachings (*Laojiao*), the New Teachings (*Xinjiao*), and even the New New Teachings (*Xinxinjiao*). These terms were not always properly understood or applied consistently by non-Muslim Chinese, and some missionaries suggested that followers of the New Teachings were members of Shi'a groups, the branch of Islam that owes its inspiration to the fourth caliph, Ali, cousin of the Prophet Muhammad. When Ali was assassinated in AD 661 the succession of the caliphate went to a rival line, the Umayyads, whose empire was ruled from Damascus. Since that time, Shi'a Muslims, followers of the Party of Ali (*Shi'a 'Ali*) from which the Shi'ites get their name, have regarded this event as a usurpation of the legitimate succession to the Prophet.

It is now generally accepted that the New Teachings and even the New New Teachings were not Shi'a sects but Sufi and Ikhwani organizations. There are in fact very few Shi'a Muslims within the borders of China, but there are two small groups: Tajiks in the Kashghar region who follow the Ismaili tradition of Shi'ism of which the Agha Khan is the spiritual leader, and a small community of Uyghurs in Yarkand county to the south-east of Kashghar who are Twelver Shi'ites, recognizing twelve principal imams as having succeeded the Prophet Muhammad and awaiting the return of the twelfth Hidden Imam who disappeared during the ninth century.

Some of the leading Chinese scholars of Islam, including Feng Jinyuan and Ma Tong, have argued convincingly that although there is little genuine Shi'a Islam in China, the influence of Shi'a culture on Sunni Islam has been subtle but profound. This effect is attributable to the influence of Persian Islam and is especially true for members of the Sufi orders. The slain caliph Ali and his wife Fatima are revered among many groups of otherwise Sunni Muslims, and many Chinese Muslims are given the names of leading Shi'a figures rather than those associated conventionally with mainstream Sunni personalities.

Nevertheless, the Sufi orders have clearly been more influential in Chinese Islam than has Shi'ism, particularly in the deeply Muslim north-west of the country. Sufism probably entered China during the later years of the Ming dynasty, although it is difficult to find reliable evidence to establish a date for its entrance. By its very nature, the mystical and often secretive heart of Islam does not leave clear traces of its movements, and there have been many attempts to demonstrate that apparently orthodox *gedimu* writings have been influenced deeply by Sufi thought. The long-lasting inspiration of Islamic movements brought to China from Persian-speaking Central Asia makes this conclusion seem plausible. As one example, Muslims in China commonly refer to their imam as *ahong*, from the Persian *akhong*.

Sufi orders or brotherhoods in China, particularly in Gansu, Ningxia, and Qinghai where they are strongest, are usually known as *menhuan*. The origins of the term *menhuan* are still imperfectly understood, but it is always assumed to correspond to the Arabic *silsila*, referring to the chain of hereditary *shaykhs* (Sufi masters) who trace their authority back to the Prophet Muhammad or his descendants. In Xinjiang, the equivalent orders are colloquially referred to as *yichan*, from the Persian *ishan* (they) and their leaders are known as *khoja*, rather than *shaykh*. In terms of doctrine and ritual they are essentially the same as the *menhuan*, but the two do not mix. *Menhuan* are for Chinese-speaking Hui, *ishan* are for Turkic speakers, primarily the Uyghurs.

There have been four main groups of Sufi orders active in China: the Khufiyya *Hufuye* and the Jahriyya *Zheherenye* or *Zhehelinye*, both branches of the Naqshbandiyya, the Qadariyya *Gadelinye*, and the Kubrawiyya *Kuburenye*. (Transcriptions into Chinese of the Arabic names of these orders have not been consistent, and so there is some variation in the spellings of the romanized Chinese.) The former two groups have their origin in the Yemen, and the latter two can be traced to Central Asia. The Sufi brotherhoods in Xinjiang also mainly belong to the Naqshbandiyya.

Like followers of the *gedimu*, members of the Sufi orders regard themselves as orthodox Sunni Muslims. The main Sufi brotherhoods trace their origins back to the great caliphs of early Islam: the Khufiyya to Abu Bakr, the Kubrawiyya to Omar, the Jahriyya to Osman, and the Qadariyya to Ali. Chinese Sufis inherited the same tradition but with some variations. Some Chinese Kubrawiyya members, influenced by Persian Shi'ism, trace their line of authority back to Fatima, the daughter of the Prophet Muhammad.

Sufism has been described as the 'intellectual cutting edge of Islam, organized in a series of monastic orders which have both enriched Islamic theology and repeatedly saved the religion from doctrinal disintegration or destruction at the hands of pagan conquerors' (Horrie and Chippindale 1990: 139). The spread of Sufism across Central Asia played

22

an important part in the strengthening and revival of Islam in China in the seventeenth and eighteenth centuries. As was the case later in the Soviet Union, Sufism may have been the crucial factor that prevented the absorption and assimilation of Hui Muslims into the Han majority, with its mixture of Confucianism, Buddhism, Daoism, and folk religions.

The *gedimu*, as the most orthodox strain of Muslims in the country, came into conflict with the Sufi movements that burgeoned in eighteenth-century China. The main doctrinal differences centred on the different emphases placed on the shariah, the Muslim code of religious law, of greatest importance to followers of the *gedimu*, and the *tariqa*, the mystical pathway, which was at the centre of the Sufi belief system. The *gedimu* doctrine put forth the view that this world and the afterlife were inseparable and that Muslims had to obtain merit in this life if they were to attain happiness in the next. This aspect of their teachings made the followers of the *gedimu* very much a sect of this world, not averse to compromise with non-Muslim authorities.

In Qing-dynasty China, this difference led to protracted conflict between *gedimu* leaders and the *shaykhs* of the Sufi orders over the *gongbei* tombs venerated by the followers of the *shaykhs*. For orthodox Muslims this practice violated the proscription on idol worship, but *gedimu* authorities generally compromised by agreeing that the tombs of saints, many of whom were of foreign origin, should be respected and that followers could visit those sites. The leaders on both sides of the argument opposed the raising of funds to build or repair the *gongbei*.

In contrast to the Sufi orders, the Shi'ites, and the followers of the *gedimu*, the Xidaotang, or Hall of the Western Pathway, is the most distinctively Chinese of all the Islamic sects active in China. Its theology is based on a number of texts written in Chinese and known collectively as the *Han ketabu*, the Han *kitab*, an interesting Sino–Muslim collocation as Han is Chinese for 'Chinese' and *kitab* (transliterated as *ketabu* in Chinese) is Arabic for 'book'. Because its followers relied primarily on religious texts translated into or written in Chinese, rather than the Arabic originals, they were sometimes known as the *Hanxuepai*, the Sinological sect.

The Languages and Literatures of Muslim China

Throughout the centuries, various languages have been used by Muslims in China. Arabic was the primary language of some of the earliest Middle Eastern traders, and it survives today in the language of religious life. Prayers, festivals, types of mosques, religious leaders, and devotional and ritual practices all have Arabic names, which are usually written in Chinese characters chosen for their sounds to replicate the pronunciation of the Arabic word (Fig. 2.1). There has been a degree of tension among Islamic scholars throughout history over the propriety of using Chinese, rather than Arabic, versions of the Koran and other sacred texts. During periods of religious revival there were frequent calls for a return to the original Arabic of the Koran, but the isolation of China's Muslim communities from the rest of the Islamic world has meant that knowledge of Arabic has been in consistent decline, even among imams, and such use has not been practical. Plate 1 shows an Arabic-language copy of the Koran, possibly dating from the sixteenth century, which is in the Xinjiang Autonomous Region Museum in Urumqi.

1. A copy of the Koran, dating from the Ming dynasty, found in Xinjiang.

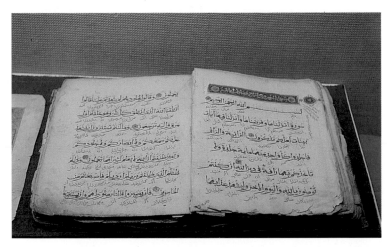

2. *Chaikhana* tea house in front of the Id Gah mosque, Kashghar.

3. The main mosque in Turpan.

4. Gathering water from the *kariz* system, Turpan.

5. Hui in the Linxia market.

6. Entrance to the Islamic Academy, Yinchuan.

7. A hall of the Great Mosque of Xi'an.

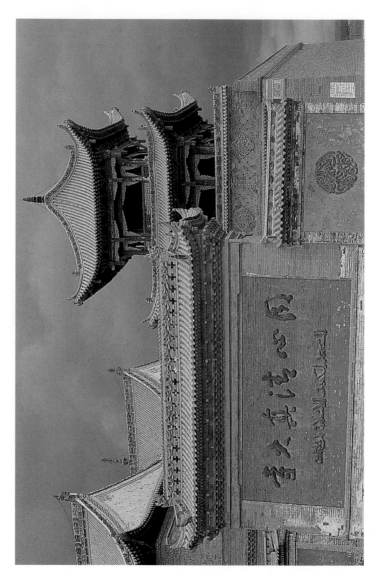

8. The Great Mosque, Tongxin.

9. Burial vault of a Sufi *shaykh*, outside the Great Mosque, Tongxin.

10. Nanguan Mosque, Yinchuan.

11. Hui boys studying in the *madrasa*, Nanguan Mosque, Yinchuan.

12. Xiguan Mosque, Yinchuan.

13. The main mosque in Najiahu, a town south of Yinchuan.

14. Façade of the Id Gah mosque, Kashghar.

15. Side chamber off the main prayer hall, Id Gah mosque, Kashghar.

16. Mosque attached to the Honglefu *daotang*, near Wuzhong, central Ningxia.

17. Small tomb of a local *shaykh*, Ningxia.

18. Fruits and spices available in the market of Wuzhong, Ningxia.

19. Commemorative wall hanging from the *hajj*, showing the Ka'ba at the Great Mosque in Mecca.

2.1 The sign on this building, in Chinese but read from right to left in Arabic fashion, gives the name of the mosque in Najiahu.

Arabic calligraphy is popular in mosques and at tomb complexes, and is sometimes seen in combination with Chinese calligraphy. In Hui areas, the Chinese and Arabic calligraphic traditions complement each other (Fig. 2.2). Arabic script is also found on signs for halal shops, food stalls, and restaurants, which makes them immediately recognizable to Muslims. Hui people are deeply attached to Arabic, which they regard as one of their languages, even though they may know little more of it than their own religious name.

The influence of Persian, which came into China alongside Arabic during the Tang dynasty and became an important lingua franca throughout the whole of the Mongol empire from China to the eastern frontiers of Europe, survives in Muslim China. Sufi orders have long been inspired by Persian texts, and even today in everyday speech a

25

2.2 The signs on this post office in Urumqi are in both Chinese and Arabic scripts.

significant number of Persian words are used in the Chinese spoken by the Hui. They habitually address one another, for example, as *dost* (friend). Persian was also very influential in the development of the vocabulary of the Uyghur language of Xinjiang. Like Uzbek, Uyghur contains a large number of Persian words, including such common ones as the names of the days of the week.

Uyghur is the main Turkic language of Xinjiang, and it is the language which non-Chinese speakers in the region use to communicate with one other. Arabic script is employed decoratively in Xinjiang as in other parts of Muslim China, but it is also used to write the Uyghur and Kazakh languages. In the 1960s, when the Chinese language was being reformed, a modified Latin script was created for Uyghur and Kazakh. This script was never popular, and the Arabic script survived in private and in religious writing. It was officially revived during the 1980s, although in a revised form which allowed for the inclusion of the vowel changes so important in Turkic languages. The retention of the Arabic script is ironic, as it creates difficulties in the contacts between Uyghurs and other Turkic speakers, particularly since their neighbours in Uzbekistan have decided to change to the Latin alphabet, which has been used in Turkey since 1928. The Uyghurs' insistence on retaining the Arabic script is an indication of the importance attached to it as a symbol of Uyghur religious and cultural identity. In Xinjiang, signs on streets, shops, and public building are normally bilingual, in Chinese and Uyghur.

For Hui Muslims, Chinese is their everyday language, although many use an extensive range of Arabic and Persian words in both speech and writing. In the remote mountain regions, literacy in Chinese has been poor, but there is also a great body of work written by Muslims in Chinese. This includes many works on Islamic theology, accounts of the *hajj* pilgrimages to Mecca, and literature, especially poetry.

3

Muslim Centres

ALTHOUGH MUSLIMS can be found throughout the whole of China, certain towns, cities, and regions have made a disproportionate contribution to the development of China's Islamic culture. Throughout the centuries, different cities have served as centres of Islam and the Muslim community. During the Tang and Song dynasties, it was Quanzhou on the south-eastern coast that was most prominent, and evidence of the importance of the Muslim quarter still survives in the carved inscriptions found there on gravestones, tomb covers, and the walls of mosques, although the town itself does not now have the same distinctive Islamic character that can be found in the towns and cities of the north-west.

Nanjing, the cosmopolitan first capital city of Ming Taizu, was a major centre of Islamic learning during the Ming dynasty, but the centre of gravity of Islamic China shifted north-west to the border areas of Gansu and Qinghai as Muslims were sent out to guard and farm the frontiers. Sufism entered north-western China and became a powerful force in the seventeenth and eighteenth centuries, and as a consequence the authority of the religious bodies of the region was reinforced and the status of Islam grew. Gathering influences from the west, the Uyghurs of southern Xinjiang were gradually converted to Islam, and by the fifteenth century the faith had spread as far east as Hami.

Xinjiang, especially the region to the south and west of the Taklamakan Desert, retains the most distinctive Muslim culture in the whole of China. This region is known to the Uyghurs as Altishahr ('six cities', after the main settlements) and to the Chinese simply as Nanjiang (Southern Xinjiang). In 1965, Xinjiang was designated the Xinjiang Uyghur Autonomous Region, in deference to the numerical superiority of the Uyghurs there. Although the level of genuine autonomy is slight, there has been some encouragement for the promotion of Uyghur culture. Islam is important to the Uyghurs both as a faith and as a part of their culture that distinguishes them from the Han Chinese, whose presence in the region many Uyghur resent as the intrusion of colonial rulers.

Kashghar

Kashghar, also known by its Chinese name Kashi, is the most important city in the Uyghur heartland of southern Xinjiang. Because of its location in the far west of the region it was regarded by travellers, both foreign and Chinese, throughout the 1950s, 1960s, and 1970s as a fabulous and unattainable destination. It is now firmly on the tourist itinerary, with modernized hotels catering to tour groups. It is also important as a garrison city, lying as it does near to China's borders with Kyrgyzstan, Tajikistan, and Afghanistan, and for this reason was closed to visitors during the Cultural Revolution and other periods of isolation. Many schools and other public buildings in the town carry signs that show they were built by the Xinjiang Production and Construction Corps, the military organization which controls much of Xinjiang's economy.

Local people are conscious of Kashgar's historical role as the capital of Yakub Beg's revolt in the 1860s, as well as the site of an independence movement of the 1930s. The city has therefore become a symbol of independent Uyghur culture and of political opposition to Chinese rule over

Xinjiang. Several major anti-Chinese demonstrations and terrorist incidents have taken place in or near Kashghar in recent years.

Traditionally, the city was divided into Chinese and Uyghur areas, and to a certain extent that division is still retained. The Chinese area of Kashghar, known before 1949 as Hancheng (Chinatown), contained Confucian and Buddhist temples and a theatre, that particular art being forbidden to strict Muslims. The appearance of the Chinese quarter today is similar to that of other Chinese urban centres, but the area around the bazaar, with the city's Id Gah mosque at its centre (see Chapter 4), is Muslim and predominantly Uyghur. It is a warren of houses, shops, metal and wood workshops, restaurants, and smaller mosques. Sheep are

traded in the square, men drink tea in the *chaikhana* tea houses (Plate 2), and traders sell vegetables from carts pulled by mules (Fig. 3.1). White-robed traders, who have travelled north from Pakistan along the Karakorum Highway, deliver copies of the Koran to backstreet bookstalls.

3.1 Traders selling vegetables in Kashghar.

The renowned Sunday bazaar takes place around the Aizilaiti Road that runs north-east from the town centre. Originally a livestock market, it has evolved into a major social event, as stockbreeders drive their sheep and cattle into the city. Each week a small town of stalls is erected, where all manner of foods and goods are sold to nomads and visitors from the outlying villages.

Kashghar's impressive Id Gah mosque is the most important symbol of Islam in Kashghar, but the city also contains the tomb of Abakh Khoja, ruler of southern Xinjiang in the seventeenth century and spiritual leader of the White Mountain sect, whose daughter was a concubine of the Qianlong emperor. South-west of the town, off the road to Tashkorgan and the Khunjerab Pass into Pakistan, lies the tomb of the man from whom Kashghar derives its name, Muhammad Kashgharli, who compiled the first dictionary of the Turkic languages in the eleventh century. The fact that his tomb is in Kashghar is important for Uyghur nationalists, who insist that Kashghar and the rest of Xinjiang are Uyghur rather than Chinese in nature.

Turpan

Turpan, also known as Turfan from Tulufan, the Chinese name for the city, is in the eastern part of Xinjiang. It is closer to China proper than is Kashghar, but is still very much a Uyghur and a Muslim city. Turpan lies in a depression well below sea level and is surrounded by relics of the region's intricate cultural history. The Buddhist cave temples of Bezeklik, with their celebrated devotional paintings, considered idolatrous and therefore badly damaged during the period of Islamization, lie to the north-east of the town. In the western outskirts of Turpan there is the ruined city of Jiaohe, which dates back to the Han dynasty (206 BC–AD 220), while further out and to the south-east are the remains of Gaochang, the two sites further testimony to the mighty pre-Islamic civilizations of Xinjiang.

Turpan has numerous mosques, one of which can be seen in Plate 3, but the city's most impressive monument to Islam is the Emin Minaret (Fig. 3.2), built on the instructions

3.2 The Emin Minaret, Turpan.

of two rulers of Turpan in the eighteenth century. Turpan is a good example of a town built on the oasis agriculture at which the Uyghurs became so expert (Plate 4). The *kariz* system of subterranean aqueducts provides the irrigation for the city (Fig. 3.3).

Linxia

Before the Muslim insurrections of the 1860s, Linxia was called Hezhou, although to Muslims it was China's Mecca or China's Little Mecca. The city lies in a frontier region with a history of war and rebellion. The population of Linxia and the countryside around it is a volatile mix of Hui and Salar Muslims, Han Chinese, and Tibetans. The

3.3 An opening of the *kariz* system, Turpan.

great Tibetan Buddhist monastery of Lhabrang lies to the south-west, and Tibetans are regular visitors to Linxia. There are many Tibetans in the town, easily distinguishable by their clothing. Monks from nearby Lhabrang and nomads from the grasslands of the high plains, come to shop for provisions, arrive in town as they have for centuries, although these days they most often come by car rather than on horseback.

The region around Linxia became important in the eighteenth century as a centre of Sufi and other dynamic Islamic orders (see Chapter 2). Like Muslim communities throughout China, the Hui of Linxia trace their origins back to the military settlers of the Yuan dynasty, who opened up new farming land while garrisoning the region. Linxia is fertile relative to most of north-west China, and it has land suitable both for agriculture and for pasturing sheep. During the Ming and Qing dynasties it emerged as one of the most concentrated areas of Hui settlement in China.

The Linxia region's claim to fame in Chinese Islam is that it was the area in which the *menhuan* system, characteristic of Chinese Islam, developed and in which the *gongbei* tomb cults emerged, as well as having played an important role in mosque education. Many mosques were built in the central Bafang area of Linxia by members of the Muslim élite intending to strengthen the influence of their *menhuan*. After making their money, usually in commerce, the wealthy Hui gentry built magnificent mansions and mosques in Bafang, which gradually emerged as a major economic, religious, and political centre for the Hui people.

Today, Linxia is the administrative centre of the Linxia Hui Autonomous Prefecture, which controls seven counties in south-western Gansu province. Linxia is approximately one hundred miles west of Lanzhou, the provincial capital of Gansu. The road to Linxia is a winding mountain trail, bumpy and with sharp hairpin bends. It is susceptible to landslides and fresh rockfalls which, having blocked part of the road during the morning hours, are likely to be being cleared by afternoon. Road improvements are beginning to reduce the isolation of Linxia. There is now a regular minibus service from Lanzhou, and a Japanese company has been constructing a toll tunnel at Qidaoliang (Seven-way bridge) which, although still incomplete at the time, was being used in September 1992. By the time the tunnel is reached, the few Han villages have petered out and it is entirely Hui territory down to the old borders of Tibet.

In Linxia itself, trade is booming. To the left of the road from Lanzhou is a spacious dealing yard with the atmosphere of a stock exchange in which hundreds of men in white caps and beards haggle noisily over live sheep and sheepskins. The Qingzhen Dasi (Great mosque) on Jiefang lu (Liberation street), just beyond the police station, is large and plain and was probably rebuilt in the 1980s. As in all predominantly Muslim towns in China, Linxia's market

3.4 Knives for sale in the Linxia market.

areas are constantly busy, with brisk trading in silks and cottons. Women in green and black veils and men in white caps throng the streets (Plate 5). Local craft products, including exquisitely decorated calabashes, lethal Hui or Bao'an knives (Fig. 3.4), carpets, and copper goods are on sale on Bei dajie (North boulevard). Many of the bookstalls in the markets and on the streets stock religious texts, both new and secondhand.

Ningxia

Before 1949, Ningxia was the name of the town in Gansu province now called Yinchuan. In 1958, Yinchuan and the rural counties that surround it were redesignated as the Ningxia Hui Autonomous Region. Approximately one-third of the population of Ningxia today are Hui Muslims, and in the mountainous south of the region whole counties are almost entirely Hui. The economy of southern Ningxia is underdeveloped and living conditions are harsh, but Hui communities have been settled there for centuries and their mosques and the tombs of their Sufi *shaykhs* are very important to the local people. In 1995 the Chinese authorities proposed that poor Hui families from the mountains should be resettled in other provinces, a plan which might help to alleviate their economic problems but would undermine their Islamic identity if it goes ahead.

Yinchuan, the administrative centre of Ningxia, has the appearance of a Han Chinese city, and there is even a square which looks like a miniature version of Beijing's Tiananmen Square, complete with gate. The main difference is the large number of mosques and the spectacular Islamic Academy. The academy was built in the 1980s, with funds provided by the Islamic Development Bank, as is acknowledged in a monument in front of the building (Fig. 3.5). It has an administrative block, a teaching block, a mosque (see Fig. 4.1), a library with books in Chinese and Arabic,

3.5 Monument in front of the Islamic Academy, Yinchuan.

and accommodation for students. The sign above the entrance to the academy (Plate 6) shows the institution's name in both Chinese and Arabic. By 1992, there were reputed to be one hundred students studying to become imams, but the campus seemed strangely empty. The Islamic Development Bank also gave financial assistance to similar academies in Beijing and Urumqi.

The further south one goes in Ningxia, the more Hui people one meets. Wuzhong is a thriving commercial centre, and in the new market the vast majority of stalls are run by Hui traders. Tongxin, further south still, has many ancient mosques. Most of Tongxin's population wear Hui dress, and the bookshops sell the Koran and prayer mats in addition to the normal books and periodicals on sale elsewhere in China. Tongxin also has an Arabic language school, built in 1985 and also funded by the Islamic Development Bank. The school is the only specialist school of Arabic in the state sector. Arabic is taught in the Islamic academies, but in Tongxin it is studied for purely secular purposes with an eye to commercial and diplomatic relations with the Middle East as north-western China emerges from decades of isolation.

Schools in the People's Republic of China are normally co-educational and this has caused some problems for the education of girls in Muslim areas. In response to this conflict with tradition, the Tongxin Girls Hui Middle School was established during the 1980s. Hui girls from the villages around Tongxin study at the school as weekly boarders, and the proportion of Hui girls in education has increased dramatically as a result. Although shy, the girls were confident enough to be able to answer questions from a stranger who had dropped in on them without warning.

4

China's Islamic Architecture

MOSQUES IN CHINA are known today as *qingzhensi* (temple of pure truth), although other terms have been used in the past—including, at times, the same words that were used for churches and synagogues, which led to a certain amount of confusion. The component parts of China's mosques are as determined by Islamic practice worldwide. All have the prayer hall with a *mihrab* alcove in the wall facing Mecca, which is intended to concentrate the attention of Muslims at prayer on the Ka'ba, the cubed building within the Great Mosque at Mecca. The hall contains, as well, the *minbar*, the platform from which the imam delivers his sermons during Friday prayers. At least one room is set aside for ritual ablutions. Depending on the size of the mosque, there may also be rooms for Koranic instruction or a more formally organized *madrasa*, a school for instruction in all aspects of Islamic life and thought, as well as guest rooms, accommodation for the imam and his staff, shops, and other buildings.

The construction style of mosques in China can vary greatly. Older mosques, many constructed during the Yuan, Ming, and early Qing dynasties, were built in a fashion very similar to the Chinese architecture of their period and were based on a timber structure. More modern constructions look to Afghanistan, Iran, the republics of the former Soviet Central Asia, or the Arab world for their models (Fig. 4.1). Since many mosques were destroyed during the Cultural Revolution, launched in 1966 and not completely ended until after Mao Zedong's death in 1976, many more examples of the newer type can now be seen.

4.1 Mosque belonging to the Islamic Academy, Yinchuan, showing the modern style of building.

The Great Mosque of Xi'an

Xi'an is primarily a Han city and is usually associated with symbols of Han Chinese imperial power such as the terracotta army and burial mound of Qin Shihuangdi, the first emperor of a unified China, and the seventh-century tomb of Emperor Tang Taizong and his consort, all of which are in the surrounding countryside. However, the city also has historical connections with Central Asia from as far back as the Tang dynasty. The city's Great Mosque, which dates back to the Yuan dynasty, is supported by a Hui community which has been present in the neighbouring Drum Tower quarter for centuries. Traditional Chinese-style mosques are laid out on the same principle as the northern Chinese *siheyuan* (courtyard house), in which rooms

39

are arranged around three sides of a quadrangle with an entrance and smaller rooms on the fourth side. Mosques constructed in the traditional manner are often based on an integrated series of courtyard buildings.

The Great Mosque provides a good example of this traditional arrangement. The grounds are comprised of a narrow rectangle, running from east to west, which is made up of a series of four linked courtyards. The hall shown in Plate 7 indicates the Chinese-style design of the architecture. The mosque, also known as the Huajue xiang (Huajue alley) Mosque or the Great Eastern Mosque, occupying an area of 12,000 square metres, is one of the largest of the traditional mosques still existing in China. Construction of the present building began in 1392, and it was refurbished during the Jiajing (1522–66) and Wanli (1573–1620) reigns of the Ming dynasty and also in the early years of the Qing dynasty. In one of the halls in the complex, surrounded with Arabic calligraphy, are the clocks used to determine the correct time of day for prayer (Fig. 4.2). There

4.2 Arabic calligraphy and clocks used to set the time for prayer in the Great Mosque, Xi'an.

are many other smaller mosques in Xi'an, but the Great Mosque has become something of a tourist attraction and foreigners, especially if they are Muslims, are likely to be taken to the site.

The Great Mosque of Tongxin

The Great Mosque of Tongxin (Plate 8) stands on high ground in the north-west quarter of the old town. From a distance the mosque looks like many traditional Buddhist temples in China, and that is precisely how the building started life. It was probably built in the fourteenth century during the Mongol occupation of China. Because it was a Mongol Lama Buddhist temple, and not a Chinese one, the structure was abandoned when the Mongols were driven out by the forces of the Ming in 1368. It was soon taken over by Muslims from Central Asia, who had earlier followed the conquering Mongol armies into China to settle in the area, and was reconsecrated as a mosque.

The building was renovated in the sixteenth century, in 1791, and again in 1907. The present structure reflects the 1907 rebuilding. More recently, it survived the Cultural Revolution, unlike many local mosques and other religious foundations throughout China, in part because, as a battered wooden notice on the wall near the entrance to the building records (Fig. 4.3), the first ethnic minority autonomous administration established with Chinese Communist Party support was organized within its walls in 1936.

According to the imam, there are normally a few dozen worshippers for daily prayers but several hundred on a Friday. During one visit, fifteen to twenty men of all ages were waiting outside the prayer hall. Behind the mosque,

4.3 This sign on the Great Mosque, Tongxin, recognizes the building as the site of the first agreement concerning minority autonomy made by the Communist forces.

in the cemetery reached through a gate in the wall, are the carefully tended shrines of two Sufi saints, or more correctly *shaykhs*, a testament to the parallel Islam which kept the faith alive when the Qing imperial government or the Communist Party tried to suppress it (Plate 9 and Fig. 4.4). From the cemetery, there is an excellent view of the town of Tongxin and of two other mosques: one a representative of the *gedimu* tradition, the other attended by members of the Jahriyya *Zheherenye* Sufi brotherhood. Today, the Great Mosque itself follows the *Yihewani* sect, the Chinese equivalent of the Ikhwani Muslim Brotherhood.

4.4 Inside the burial vault of a Sufi *shaykh*, behind the Great Mosque, Tongxin.

The Nanguan Mosque, Yinchuan

The Nanguan (South gate) Mosque (Plate 10) is the largest in Yinchuan and is a good example of a modern mosque constructed after the Cultural Revolution in a Middle Eastern or Central Asian style. This technique does not use a wooden framework, as is found in the older Chinese-style mosques, and the most prominent feature is the large green dome which tops the structure. The layout avoids the Chinese linked courtyards and is instead based on a more centralized design.

The Nanguan Mosque is on two levels (Fig. 4.5), with the main prayer hall on the upper level and on the lower level separated washing facilities for men and women, a small prayer hall, a resting room for the *ahongs*, and a guest room. The decoration, as is typical of this category of mosque, aims to be simple yet elegant, with few carvings or paintings. In the courtyard is a shop where the Koran and other devotional materials are on sale. On the

4.5 Entrance to the Nanguan Mosque, Yinchuan.

4.6 Photomontage showing the destruction and rebuilding of the Nanguan Mosque, Yinchuan.

wall of the shop is a montage of photographs (Fig. 4.6) depicting the destruction of the building in the mid-1960s, the makeshift prayer hall made up of mats and tables that the congregation used on the site, and the reconstruction of the mosque in a Middle Eastern style in the mid-1980s. In March 1991 it was fully active, with a madrasa in which a dozen or so boys could be seen reading aloud from the Koran (Plate 11).

Also in Yinchuan, the Xiguan (West gate) Mosque was rebuilt in 1981 in a Middle Eastern style (Plate 12). According to the *ahong*, the original building was constructed in the 1880s. He had taken part in the *hajj* in 1987, and one other *ahong* had also been to Mecca. His congregation numbered approximately one hundred worshippers on ordinary days but over three hundred on Fridays. In Yinchuan there are twelve or so mosques, most of which were destroyed in the Cultural Revolution and rebuilt beginning in the 1980s.

Construction of mosques continues in Yinchuan and a new mosque, the Xincheng Nanmen (New town south gate) Mosque on Mancheng Street South, was being built in

September 1992 (Fig. 4.7). South of Yinchuan, in the village of Najiahu (the Na family village), the main mosque is in the old Chinese style (Plate 13). Parts of it were destroyed during the Cultural Revolution, but the main prayer hall and some of the outlying buildings remain intact.

4.7 Construction of the Xincheng Nanmen Mosque, Yinchuan.

The Id Gah Mosque, Kashghar

There are important differences between the mosques of Xinjiang and those of the Muslim communities in China proper. The differences stem, in part, from the much greater concentration of Muslims in Xinjiang, where daily life has revolved around mosque activities for centuries. In addition, the distinctive Uyghur culture of Xinjiang influences the style and practices of Islam. Kashghar is said to have had over 12,000 mosques at the time of the foundation of the People's Republic in 1949, but the majority of these were destroyed during the Cultural Revolution. Rebuilding during the 1980s has brought the number back to more than 6,000, and now every street or lane seems to have at least one mosque.

Because of the number of Muslims in Xinjiang, and the fact that mosques were important for so many aspects of their lives, different categories of mosque with different functions have evolved. Xinjiang mosques are classified in five groups. *Id Gah* mosques (the name is taken from the Arabic word for festival and the Persian for place) are the largest, and are the locations where the main religious festivals are celebrated. They tend to be the most lavishly constructed. *Jami'* (assembly) mosques, also known as *Juma* (Friday) mosques, are the next largest and are situated in areas where there are substantial communities of Muslims. *Masjid* are the small mosques found in every street and lane in towns and villages throughout Xinjiang and are used for daily prayers. *Mazar* mosques are attached to the *mazar* or tomb of a Sufi or other saint. Finally, there are the *yatim* (orphan) mosques scattered about the steppe, in the desert, or by the side of the road. They have no staff but are available to the passing Muslim for prayer.

The first Id Gah mosque in Kashghar is said have been built in 1442, but the present structure dates back only as far as the nineteenth century (Plate 14). The building was rebuilt in its present form in 1874 during the rebel regime of Yakub Beg. It is the largest mosque in China: its prayer hall alone has an area of more than 2,500 square metres and is said to be able to hold ten thousand worshippers. In September 1992, after visiting Beijing and Urumqi, President Hashemi Rafsanjani of Iran visited Kashghar and led the prayers in the Id Gah mosque, underlining the importance of the mosque to China's Muslims. Plate 15 shows the overspill area for the main prayer hall, a view which may give some indication of the size of the building.

Tombs

Mosques provide the most obvious examples of Islamic architecture, but in north-western China shrines built around the tombs of the masters of Sufi orders and other religious leaders are at least as important to ordinary worshippers. They are known in Chinese-speaking areas as *gongbei*, a term which is derived from the Arabic *qubba* (dome or cupola), as the dome is often a prominent feature of the shrines (Fig. 4.8). In Xinjiang, the same monument is known as a *mazar*, the Uyghur word for grave. The tomb shrines are objects of profound veneration to their devotees, and many have developed into major religious centres (*daotang* in Chinese), with prayer halls, schools, and lodgings for visitors.

4.8 Domed tombs on the hills outside the ruined city of Jiaohe, near Turpan.

47

The Honglefu *daotang* of the Zheherenye (Jahriyyah) Sufi *menhuan* at Wuzhong, in Ningxia (Plate 16), provides a good illustration of the tomb cult of the Chinese-speaking Hui Muslims. The present Honglefu complex has a *daotang*, *gongbei*, garden, guest rooms, bathhouse, kitchen, and accountant's office. The Zheherenye order is the largest of the *menhuan* in China and has followers throughout the whole of the country, from Yunnan, to the central provinces of Hebei and Henan, to Shandong on the east coast. Its founder was Ma Mingxin (1719–81), who was from Wudu in Gansu province. On his return to China from the *hajj*, Ma preached in Xunhua and came into conflict with the leaders of the *gedimu* branch of Islam. He was executed in prison in Lanzhou in 1781 during a period of bitter conflict between Muslim groups.

Honglefu *daotang* is a few miles north-west of the town of Jinjibao and is controlled by the descendants of Ma Hualong. Jinjibao was one of the centres of the 1869 Hui uprising, and Ma Hualong was one of the rebel leaders in the town and the man regarded by Zuo Zongtang, the pre-eminent military leader opposing the Muslim uprising, as the most serious threat to imperial power. Zuo had Ma executed on 2 March 1871, along with his son, Ma Yaobang, and more than eighty other rebel leaders. According to local tradition, Ma Hualong was buried at Honglefu and a *gongbei* established there (Fig. 4.9). Although Jinjibao was obliterated after the Hui rebellion, the site of the rising and Ma Hualong's tomb are sacred to the Hui people of the region. In the 1980s Honglefu regained its importance as a religious centre. Thousands of followers of the Zheherenye sect from Yunnan, Xinjiang, and elsewhere congregated there during major religious festivals to continue the *menhuan* tradition, staying either in the residential part of the *daotang* or in the houses of local villagers.

4.9 Site reputed to hold the graves of the Hui rebel leader Ma Hualong and his son, Ma Yaobang, at the Honglefu *daotang*, near Wutong, Ningxia.

Not all tomb shrines are on such a large scale as the Honglefu complex. High in the picturesque Helanshan range, to the west of the Yellow River in Ningxia (Plate 17), there is a small tomb to a local *shaykh*. It backs directly onto a small Buddhist temple, a good example of the religious complexity of the region.

5

Daily Life in Muslim China

MUSLIMS IN CHINA can often be distinguished by their clothing and headwear. In the reputedly egalitarian days of the Cultural Revolution, all distinctions of dress were discouraged and Muslim men and women tended to dress in the regulation *Zhongshan zhuang*, the plain military-style suit worn by Sun Yatsen and popularized by Mao Zedong. Since Mao's death in 1976, differences in clothing have become more common and ethnic groups have again taken to asserting their cultural distinctiveness in their clothing.

Hui men are easily distinguishable by the white or, less frequently, blue peakless caps that they wear. There is a tradition that the blue-capped Hui are the descendants of groups of Chinese Jews who assimilated into the Hui rather than the Han when their numbers became few. Not all Hui men wear the distinctive caps: they are more common in the countryside than in the larger cities and more common among farmers than the educated. Hui men who do not normally wear a cap may well keep one handy to put on when they visit the mosque. In Xinjiang, Uyghur men and boys favour colourful embroidered square caps known as flower caps, while Kazakh and Kyrgyz men prefer tall fur or felt hats or caps. Han men wear head covering less often than do Muslims, although this naturally varies with climate and season.

The head covering worn by women varies considerably in the same way that it does in all Muslim societies. There are regional differences which mark out the influences of local culture, differences according to social status, and differences in the way the Koranic injunction to dress

5.1 Hui women and men in Linxia.

modestly is interpreted. Educated Hui women in Beijing and other large cities may well not cover their heads at all, while in the rural areas and in southern Xinjiang, the veil in one form or another is almost universal.

In Linxia, the old Hui rebel stronghold of Hezhou, unmarried women wear short green headscarves and married women short black ones (Fig. 5.1). In Ningxia, and especially in Tongxin and the south of the region, women wear a white head and neck covering (Fig. 5.2). In eastern Xinjiang, including Turpan and Urumqi, many women wear long, brightly coloured scarves around their heads, a fashion similar to that of the former Soviet Central Asia. In Kashghar and the rest of southern Xinjiang, the bastion of traditional Uyghur culture, a full red-brown veil which covers the whole of the head and face is common (Fig. 5.3), although many younger women do not veil themselves. Uyghur women, in common with their Uzbek neighbours, favour light, brightly coloured dresses and skirts, often white with flashes of orange, blue, and green.

51

5.2 Women traders in Tongxin wearing the white head covering characteristic of the region.

Beards are an important cultural marker for Muslim men. Few Han Chinese men wear beards today, although they are part of the image of the Daoist patriarch. For members of certain Sufi orders, beards are of special significance. Sufis of the Jahriyya orders tend to shave the sides of their beards in memory of their founding *shaykh*, Ma Mingxin. The imperial Chinese troops who killed Ma in 1781 shaved off his beard before executing him. Although by no means universal, beards are far more common among older Kazakh and Kyrgyz men than among the Chinese in general.

Muslims in China have personal names which can distinguish them from the Han majority. For Uyghurs and the other non-Chinese speakers of Xinjiang, these names in their own languages clearly mark them out from the Han. Prominent Uyghurs in recent years include the politician Ismail Aimat and the writer Turghun Almas, whose names are characteristic of their Turkic roots.

Hui Muslims, on the other hand, have names in the traditional Chinese form: that is, a surname, monosyllabic with a very few exceptions, followed by a given name of one or two syllables. Examples of this form are Wang Daiyu and Ma Tong. Hui also have a religious or Koranic name, derived from the Arabic, which they place before their Chinese name and which they may or may not use when dealing with non-Muslims. Mahmud Ma Xiao and Sharif Wang Yongliang are two examples of these combined names. During the Cultural Revolution, these religious names were little used outside family and Muslim circles, but they gradually began to reappear on business cards during the 1980s.

Certain surnames are common among the Hui, such as Ma, probably derived from the first syllable of Muhammad, and Na and Ding, which both come from the name Nasruddin. However, it should not be assumed that every

5.3 Uyghur woman and man in front of the Id Gah mosque, Kashghar.

Chinese with these surnames is Muslim, and Chinese Muslims may well have surnames, such as Yang, which are also common among non-Muslim Chinese.

Food and Drink

The Chinese cuisine familiar to many Westerners has spread into the Muslim areas of China with the expansion of the Han population, but the ethnic minority groups all have their own traditions of eating and drinking and there are many hybrid foods and drinks. Chinese writers have left records of exotic Central Asian and Indian fruits, vegetables, and spices encountered as the Tang empire expanded westwards into the lands of the Turkic peoples during the seventh and eighth centuries. Over the centuries, a distinctive halal tradition has evolved among the Muslims of China. In general, recipes were not written down but were passed by word of mouth from generation to generation of specialist chefs. In the 1950s, many of the traditional recipes from this oral tradition were collected and written down for the first time, and cookery books were published with titles such as *Chinese Halal Recipes*, *The Hui Cookbook*, *Complete Mutton Recipes*, and *Beijing Snacks*. These texts included recipes for many local Halal dishes that had previously only been known in one neighbourhood.

Although it is usually assumed that rice is the most common staple food in China, wheat and millet are grown widely in the north, and northern Chinese of all ethnic groups often eat bread and noodles of various kinds in preference to rice. Han Chinese eat bread in the form of *mantou*, steamed rolls, and *mianbao*, baked bread, but the further west one goes, the more common it is to see shops

54

and street stalls with stacks of thick hard bread baked after the fashion of northern India and Afghanistan. This bread, *nan* in the Uyghur language as in Urdu, Hindi, and Persian, is the staple food of Xinjiang, and the *nan* stall (Fig. 5.4) is a common feature in towns as far east as Xi'an.

5.4 *Nan* stall, Xi'an.

The meat of choice in the Muslim areas is, not surprisingly, different from that of the rest of China. Chinese cooks make much use of chicken and pork, but the latter is, of course, prohibited to Muslims. In north-west China, lamb or mutton is ubiquitous, sheep-rearing being the most effective way of making a living in the infertile mountain valleys. Roast mutton with a spicy baste that has a taste somewhere between Indian tandoori and Chinese five-spice flavours is the basis for many restaurant meals, and the most sumptuous Uyghur banquets feature a whole roast sheep covered with the same spiced glaze. Kebab (*kewap* to the Uyghurs) stalls can be found on the streets of Xi'an and in the covered Uyghur bazaars and the parks of Urumqi.

5.5 *Kewap* stall, Xi'an.

Figure 5.5 depicts a *kewap* stall on the streets of Xi'an: the stallholder is wearing the characteristic embroidered cap of the Uyghurs.

Kebabs, and other mutton dishes in north-western China, have a distinct flavour which is derived from the use of spices similar to aniseed. In the Erdaoqiao bazaar in downtown Urumqi, rival kebab vendors, all young Uyghur men, call out to attract customers who sit on benches in front of the grill to eat the kebabs. If a customer does not order what the stallholder considers to be a sufficient quantity of kebabs, the stallholder may throw the tendered money on the floor in disdain. Uyghur and Hui chefs have made kebabs popular even in conservative Beijing, although some Han Chinese claim to dislike lamb which they describe as having a rank flavour or *shanweir* (hilly taste). Mutton is associated in the minds of many Han with frontier peoples such as the Uyghurs and Mongols, and this association may be part of the reason for its unpopularity.

Favoured restaurant fare in Gansu's Linxia Hui Autonomous Prefecture is *lamian*, a bowl of thick broad

56

noodles in a spicy beef stew, served in Linxia with a degree of courtesy and attentiveness rarely found in Han restaurants. This dish is also known as *laghman* to the Uyghurs and Kazakhs and is on the menu of many restaurants in Xinjiang and Kazakhstan.

A dish of mutton and rice also popular in Xinjiang is known to the Uyghurs as *polo*. It is the equivalent to pilau or pilaf in Indian or Turkish cuisine. The Han Chinese rather discourteously translate this as *zhuafan* ('grab food'), because it is eaten with the tips of the fingers rather than with chopsticks. Uyghurs also favour bread buns filled with a mixture of minced mutton and onion and baked in the ovens that are used for the *nan* bread. These are called *samsa* in the Uyghur language, a word related to the Indian samosa. Cultural links between western Xinjiang and northern India and Pakistan are not surprising in that, in spite of the difficult terrain, there was until late in this century regular caravan trade through the passes in the Karakorum mountains, and Uyghur merchants from Yarkand and Kashghar were regular visitors to Srinagar.

Further east, in Xi'an, the speciality at the halal Moon and Stars restaurant on Beiyuanmen lu (Fig. 5.6) is *yangrou paomo*, a dish and a style of cooking which seems completely alien to the usual image of Chinese cuisine. Each customer is given a huge bowl and several crisp flat breads similar to the *nan* of Pakistan, Afghanistan, and Xinjiang but known in Chinese as *nang*. The bread is crumbled into the bowl in pieces as small as possible. The bowl is then taken away by the waiters and filled to the brim with a thick lamb broth. These few examples give only a taste of the variety of fare found in the halal cuisine of China.

Alcohol is, of course, forbidden to pious Muslims, but Chinese Muslim communities are not as strict in their observance of this prohibition as in some other parts of the

5.6 The Moon and Stars, a halal restaurant in Xi'an.

Islamic world, and Ningxia, Gansu, and Xinjiang all produce thin, weak bottled beers which are widely consumed. In recent years Yining beer has even been exported to Kazakhstan by Kazakh pedlars and is on sale in the street markets of Almaty. Nevertheless, the most common drink among Muslims is tea, and in Xinjiang, particularly in the south of the region, the *chaikhana*, or tea house, is the most popular place for men to drink, eat, and relax. Around the square in front of the Id Gah mosque in Kashghar are several *chaikhana* which serve tea and fruit and provide benches where customers can sit, drink, talk, and watch television under an awning to shelter them from the blistering sun. In Ningxia, tea is drunk sweet with added herbs and dried fruits. The pinnacle of this tradition is *babao gaiwan cha* (Eight treasures covered-bowl tea)(Fig. 5.7). Tea infused with sugar, herbs, spices, and fruits is drunk from a mug with a lid, the lid being used to hold back the residue of flavouring while the liquor is drunk. Muslims in Lanzhou and its environs favour tea with milk in the fashion that the British learned in India.

Although the north-west, where the most traditional Muslim communities are found, is considered to be the poorest region in China, the deficiencies in grain and vegetable production are compensated for to some extent by the wealth of fruit that the region produces. Honey-sweet Hami melons, as well as the white seedless grapes from Turpan which are grown on vines stretched across frames throughout the city, are famed throughout China. The Turpan grapes are dried as sultanas and used as the raw material for the sugary wines of the region. Markets throughout the north-west of China are bursting with fresh and dried fruits. Plate 18 shows the rich variety of dried fruits and spices available in the largely Hui market of Wuzhong in Ningxia.

The Working Life of China's Muslims

Muslim citizens of China can be found in all walks of life: there are Hui and Uyghur teachers, academics, politicians, police officers, and soldiers, and many Muslims work along

5.7 *Babao gaiwan cha* (Eight treasures covered-bowl tea).

side non-Muslim colleagues. Certain occupations, however, are particularly associated with one or another Muslim group, especially in the north-west. The relative poverty of the north-west is largely the result of geographical factors. Vast stretches of land are desert, and there is little low-lying land suitable for growing the main arable crops such as rice or wheat, although both are grown in the area. The isolation of the region from the rich and powerful provinces of China proper has until recently restricted trade and investment from outside.

In Xinjiang, the traditional economy was dominated by livestock-rearing, and there are still about 35 million head of livestock, primarily sheep, in the region. While the Uyghurs have been settled oasis farmers for centuries, nomadic pastoralism was also practised, especially by the Kazakhs, who moved their flocks great distances from season to season, crossing what are now the borders of China and Kazakhstan. Oasis agriculture has been very important given the natural circumstances of the settlements, and the sophisticated system of *kariz* wells and canals was constructed to tap melting snow from the Tianshan range and to transfer the water to settlements such as Turpan. This system is used throughout Central Asia as far west as Turkmenistan and may have been begun by Iranian captives based on the similar *qanat* irrigation used in Iran.

Grain and cotton are grown in Xinjiang, and today there are modern cotton factories including a Japanese joint-venture business in Changji, a town north of Urumqi, which uses the most up-to-date technology. Apart from the oases, agriculture remains underdeveloped because of the serious irrigation problems in the grasslands and deserts, as well as the constant threat of extended drought. Fruit-growing is important to the region, and both tinned and dried fruit are exported. The wine made from Turpan grapes is too syrupy for most Western tastes, but it is potentially of high quality.

In the Hui areas of Ningxia and south-western Gansu, hill farming is still the foundation of the rural economy. Sheep are again the mainstay of rural life, but there are also vegetable plots with some land given over to arable farming and even a small amount of rice produced in low-lying areas such as the Yellow River valley in central Ningxia. Because agriculture can only supply part of the needs of the local population, crafts and trade are very important to the economy. In the traditional Chinese value system loosely designated as Confucianism, handicrafts and especially commerce were at the bottom of the social scale; society extolled the virtue of the scholar and the peasant. The reality was rather different from the rhetoric—fine handicraft goods were produced in cities such as the porcelain centre of Jingdezhen and the silk-producing town of Suzhou and were traded around the nation—but merchants were often made to feel that their calling was a pariah career.

Attitudes towards craftsmanship in the Muslim communities of China are very different from those of the Han majority. The Muslims have a craft tradition which goes back six centuries: the facility that Central Asians had in the decorative arts, building, and craftsmanship in general was one of the main reasons that the Mongol conquerors originally had brought them eastwards into China. This tradition of craftsmanship continues today. Examples can be found in the embroidery of the Uyghurs, in particular their multicoloured *doppa* hats and embroidered bags. There is also a long tradition of carpet-making in cities like Hotan and Kashghar (Fig. 5.8).

In present-day Kashghar, many Uyghurs take pride in the fact that the majority of those who live in the centre of

5.8 Carpet-finishing, Kashghar.

the city are self-employed, rather than employees of state enterprises. The pride is not so much connected with social status as it is an expression of their independence from the alien Chinese state. The Uyghurs excel as manufacturers of copper and tinware (Fig. 5.9), and produce many local handicrafts, such as traditional musical instruments, which are rapidly becoming an important source of income since trade and tourism have expanded via Urumqi and along the Karakorum Highway (Fig. 5.10).

The Hui have developed a reputation as astute traders, especially in high-value goods such as jewellery, spices, and perfumes. Their reputation for mercantile expertise, which they retain to this day, complemented the Muslim crafts tradition perfectly and gave the Hui an occupational niche in Chinese society. Confucianism abhorred commerce, but to Muslims it is an honourable occupation, a calling fol-

lowed by the Prophet Muhammad in his early years, as
well as by his father and the uncle, Abu Talib, who raised
him. Sheep are the core of rural commerce in north-
western China today and are important also in the urban
areas. In addition to the market of Linxia, on the Tibetan
marches, where the traveller is greeted by the sight of hundreds of nearly identically dressed Hui men bartering over
sheep carcasses, live sheep are also traded in the bazaar
area of Kashghar in front of the great Id Gah mosque.

Butchery has also become a specialist Hui occupation,
which helps to ensure the production of halal meat under
religious supervision. The Hui businessman Hajji Wang
Chunxuan, from Wuzhong, had become a millionaire by
1991 by buying sheepskins from the hill farmers and selling them to be processed into sheepskin rugs for the Japanese
market. His new house was home to fifteen members of

5.9 Uyghur tinsmith, central Kashghar.

5.10 Uyghur woodcarver's stall, central Kashghar.

his family. The traditional northern Chinese *kang* in his living room was decorated with tiles. Above it was a commemorative wall hanging from Mecca with the Ka'ba, the venerated cube-shaped building in the Great Mosque of Mecca, at its centre (Plate 19).

6

Islam and the Chinese State

RELATIONS BETWEEN MUSLIMS and the state in China have been strained for centuries. In the view of the imperial government of the Qing dynasty, Muslims were mutinous subjects who had periodically to be subdued by force. More recently, the People's Republic has had a complex relationship with its Muslim citizens. It has attempted to placate both Hui and Turkic Muslims by creating autonomous regions in which the minorities have been given some influence over the government of the areas in which they are a significant proportion of the population. The Cultural Revolution tarnished this policy, however, as ethnic and religious minorities bore the brunt of the attacks by Red Guards on buildings, customs, and beliefs that did not conform to the simplistic peasant ideas of normality fostered by Mao. In the two decades since Mao's death and the beginning of Deng Xiaoping's drive to build a modern economy, the economic potential of the ethnic minorities has been recognized, and the Communist Party has encouraged greater toleration of their religious practices.

For China's Muslims, this increased tolerance has meant permission to rebuild mosques that were destroyed during the 1960s and even leeway to build completely new ones. The number allowed to take part in the *hajj* pilgrimage to Mecca increases every year, although the state still attempts, through the Islamic Association of China, to control this potentially disruptive interchange with other Muslims. The official view appears to be that as long as Islam in China does not conflict with the interests of the state, it is in the interest of the state to encourage it. This is seen as good publicity for China in its diplomatic relations with its near neighbours Pakistan and Iran, as well as with the countries of the Middle East, and the government has taken pains to invite international Islamic delegations to China to demonstrate that Muslims in China are as free to practise their religion as in other Muslim countries.

Since Islam does not always recognize the separation of the spiritual and the secular, there are inevitably areas of profound conflict between the Chinese state and its Muslim citizens. This conflict is at its most intense when religion is fused with nationalism. Whatever policy changes the Chinese Communist Party makes, there is one principle that appears to be irrevocable: the territorial integrity of China. In Chinese texts, China is regularly referred to as *Shenzhou*, the Sacred Land, rather than the prosaic *Zhongguo*, Middle Kingdom. This attachment to the territory that Qing-dynasty China occupied at its height in the eighteenth century has fuelled many of the conflicts between ethnic minorities and the Chinese state since 1949. Ethnic and religious minorities within China have been granted concessions, but the one concession that they cannot be permitted is genuine independence. This difference is at the heart of the much-publicized conflict between Beijing and many Tibetans, and it is also a long-running problem in Xinjiang, where part of the population insists on the need for an independent Eastern Turkestan. In serious disturbances that have taken place in Xinjiang in the 1990s, the forces of Islam and Turkic nationalism have frequently combined. It is just this combination that the government in Beijing most fears.

Glossary

ahong
The most common term used for the imam among Hui Muslims; derived from the Persian *akhond* (teacher or preacher).

autonomous region
An administrative division of the People's Republic of China, generally equivalent to a province but intended to demonstrate a greater degree of autonomy for its ethnic minority population. Autonomous prefectures and counties also exist within provinces and autonomous regions.

chaikhana
A tea house. The term is used in the Uygar and Persian languages.

gedimu
The main stream of orthodox Muslims in China; from the Arabic, *al-Qadim* (the ancient).

gongbei
Tombs in north-west China which are the object of veneration by Sufi and other orders.

Great Leap Forward
Mao Zedong's 1958 mass mobilization to achieve modernization and industrialization at great speed, which was followed by widespread famine and the death of millions.

halal
Permitted according to Islamic law; often used to refer to meat slaughtered and prepared in keeping with religious standards.

Han
The majority population of China, as distinguished from those classified as ethnic minorities.

Ikhwani
Associated with the fundamentalist Muslim Brotherhood, formed in Egypt in 1929.

imam
The leader of the congregation at a mosque.

Ka'ba	The cube-shaped shrine in Mecca which is the focus of the daily prayers of all Muslims.
madrasa	An Islamic religious school, usually attached to a mosque.
mazar	The Uyghur equivalent of the *gongbei* tombs.
menhuan	Hereditary Sufi or other mystical orders among the Hui people.
mihrab	A niche in the wall of a mosque indicating the direction of Mecca.
minbar	The pulpit or platform in a mosque's prayer hall from which the imam delivers the sermon.
qingzhensi	Meaning 'temple of pure truth', the most common Chinese term for a mosque.
shariah	The body of Islamic religious law.
shaykh	A term, meaning 'elder', used for the leaders of Sufi and other brotherhoods.
Shi'a	In full *Shi'a 'Ali* (the Party of Ali), an alternative tradition within Islam that is of particular importance in Iran and parts of Central Asia and is separate from the majority Sunni tradition.
Sino-Soviet dispute	The split between the Communist super-powers that began in 1960, led to border conflicts in 1969, and divided many Central Asian Muslim communities.
Sufism	A mystical and often secretive side of Islam that has played a key role in keeping alive the religion at times of repression.
Sunni	The orthodox or mainstream tradition in world Islam.
tariqa	The Sufi path or order.

Selected Bibliography

There is still very little reliable and up-to-date material written in English on Muslims in China and, consequently, most of the information for this book has been obtained in China or from Chinese-language sources. The following, however, may be of interest for further reading.

Allworth, Edward, ed. (1989), *Central Asia: 120 Years of Russian Rule* (rev. edn.), Durham, N. C.: Duke University Press.

Bonavia, Judy (1992), 'Introduction', in *The Silk Road*, Hong Kong: Odyssey Guides.

Broomhall, Marshall (1910), *Islam in China: A Neglected Problem*, London: Darf.

Chu Wen-djang (1966), *The Moslem Rebellion in Northwest China, 1862–1878*, The Hague: Mouton.

Dreyer, June Teufel (1976), *China's Forty Millions: Minority Nationalities and National Integration in the People's Republic of China*, Cambridge, Ma.: Harvard University Press.

Forbes, Andrew D. W. (1986), *Warlords and Muslims in Chinese Central Asia: A Political History of Republican Sinkiang 1911–1949*, Cambridge: Cambridge University Press.

Gladney, Dru C. (1991), *Muslim Chinese: Ethnic Nationalism in the People's Republic*, Cambridge, Ma.: Council on East Asian Studies, Harvard University.

Holledge, Simon (1988), *Collins Illustrated Guide to Xi'an*, London: Collins.

Horrie, Chris and Chippindale, Peter (1990), *What is Islam?*, London: Star.

Israeli, Raphael (1980), *Muslims in China: A Study in Cultural Confrontation*, London: Curzon Press.

Journal of the Institute of Muslim Minority Affairs, published by the Institute for Muslim Minority Affairs in Jeddah, South Arabia.

Lattimore, Owen (1962), *Inner Asian Frontiers of China*, Boston: Beacon Press.

Li Shujiang (1994), *Mythology and Folklore of the Hui, a Muslim Chinese People*, Albany, N. Y.: State University of New York Press.

Ma Yin et al., eds., trans. (1989), *China's Minority Nationalities*, Beijing: Foreign Languages Press.

Mackerras, Colin (1994), *China's Minorities: Integration and Modernization in the Twentieth Century*, Hong Kong: Oxford University Press.

Whittell, Giles (1993), *Central Asia: The Practical Handbook*, London: Cadogan.

Index

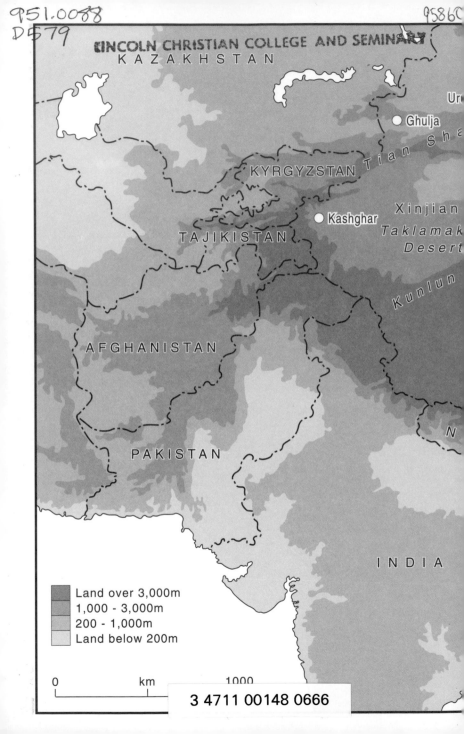

KAZAKHSTAN

Ur

● Ghulja

Tian Sha

KYRGYZSTAN

Xinjian

● Kashghar

Taklamak
Desert

TAJIKISTAN

Kunlun

AFGHANISTAN

N

PAKISTAN

INDIA

Land over 3,000m
1,000 - 3,000m
200 - 1,000m
Land below 200m

0   km   1000